A FAM

To

Minnesota's North Shore

Nancy Hereid and Eugene D. Gennaro

with Allen D. Glenn, Steven Rakow,
Gerald C. Backlund, Bruce Munson,
Mary Jo Olson, and Nancy J. Berini

Updated and revised by Alice Tibbetts

Third printing, 1993
Published by Minnesota Sea Grant

© Minnesota Sea Grant
University of Minnesota

ISBN 0-9638011-0-4

Lake Superior was named "Kitche Gummi," or great water, by the Ojibwa Indians and "Superieur" by the early French explorers because of its position at the head, or top, of all the Great Lakes.

Contents

Private facilities are not included in this book. To find out more about private facilities along the shore, contact local chambers of commerce; the information centers in Duluth, Two Harbors, Silver Bay, and Grand Marais; or other associations, such as the Minnesota Arrowhead Association, Tip of the Arrowhead Association, or the Lutsen/Tofte Tourism Association.

For information on Minnesota State Parks, festivals and other attractions, contact the Department of Tourism.

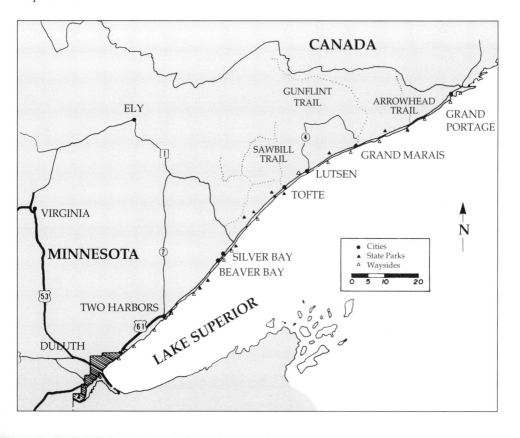

The road from Duluth to the Pigeon River at the Canadian border follows 147 miles of pebble beaches, rocky cliffs, expansive forests, and quaint towns. You'll see Lake Superior's indelible imprint on the people and places you visit. This guide will introduce you to historic places, unique environments, and the sheer beauty of the North Shore. Suggested activities in this book will add to your understanding of the area and the enjoyment of your journey.

Lake Superior has a calming fascination, whether you visit Minnesota's North Shore or live here year-round. From the sun shimmering calm of July to the gray crashing waves of November, the lake is a living presence that helps shape the climate, landscape, economy, and the quality of life along the shore. Here are a few facts about Lake Superior to help you appreciate the greatness of this inland Sea.

Facts about Lake Superior

Lake Superior covers 31,280 square miles: the area covered by Massachusetts, Connecticut, Rhode Island, Vermont, and New Hampshire combined. It's the greatest Great Lake, the largest lake in the world by surface area, and the second largest by volume. Mile-deep Lake Baikal in Siberia contains the greatest volume of freshwater.

Drive the interstate between Chicago and Cleveland for a good idea of Lake

Is Lake Superior as polluted as the other Great Lakes?

Answer on page 47

hole, with only a few floors above water.

Just how much water is in Lake Superior? The lake contains three quadrillion gallons (3,000,000,000,000,000). That's ten percent of the world's fresh surface water–half of the water in the Great Lakes–enough water to flood Canada, the U.S., Mexico, and South America with one foot of water. A child born today would be 20 years old before the Mississippi River's flow into the Gulf of Mexico would equal the amount of water in Lake Superior.

Lake Superior's drainage basin is small for the size of the lake: 49,300 square miles compared to 1.2 million square miles for the Mississippi River. Each year, 2.5 feet of water falls directly on the lake as rain or snow. Two more feet enters the lake each year through streams or groundwater.

Lake Superior does not have tides, but weather produces a tidal-like rise and fall called a seiche (saysh). Whereas the gravitational pull of the sun and moon cause tides, persistent strong winds accompanying a high pressure system "pile-up" water against the lake's windward shore to begin a seiche. Like water in a pan that's been tipped then laid flat, the water rebounds to the opposite shore. The rise and fall sloshing of the water continues after the weather conditions causing it have passed. Lake Superior seiches rarely affect the water level more than one foot.

Superior's length, 350 miles. Do the same between Duluth and Minneapolis for an appreciation of its width, 160 miles. If Lake Superior's shoreline was unraveled into a straight line highway, you could travel 1,826 miles, from Duluth to Miami. It would take 2,351 ore ships placed end to end to form a line from Duluth to the eastern end of the lake at Sault St. Marie, Michigan.

Lake Superior is so big, it takes the sun 30 minutes to travel across the lake. As orange twilight fades to purple dusk at Sault St. Marie, the sun still casts long shadows in Duluth.

Lake Superior is also the deepest of the Great Lakes. Much of the shoreline drops off quickly and sharply to an average lake-wide depth of 489 feet. Along much of the North Shore, the lake depth drops to 700 feet within three miles of shore. The lake's deepest spot of 1,333 feet is forty miles off the Michigan shore near Munising. The world's tallest building, the Chicago Sears Tower, could fit in that

Lester River to Two Harbors

Lester River

The Ojibwa Indians named the river "Busabiki-zibi," a river that flows though a worn hollow in the rock.

The mouth of the Lester River is a popular spot for smelt fishing during the spring run of this small, silvery fish.

On the rocky shore along the mouth of this river you can see evidence of the scraping action of glaciers. They moved through this area in a southwest direction about 14,000 years ago.

One block north of Lester River is the U.S. Environmental Protection Agency water quality laboratory. Group tours are possible with advance notice.

Shortly beyond Lester River, follow the turn-off signs to the Lake Superior North Shore Drive, which follows the shoreline to Two Harbors.

The extensive stands of aspen along the shore from Lester River to Knife River are evidence of forest fires that occurred in 1918.

Try This at Lester River

Try to find the scratches or grooves (not the cracks) on the rock at the mouth of the Lester River. These grooves were made by glaciers before the lake was formed.

Do the scratches go in the same direction as the shoreline or do they follow the path of the river? Is this rock easy to scratch? Try it. How much force do you think it took to make these scratches?

Glacial grooves on rocks at the mouth of the Lester River

Lumberjacks in woods near Two Harbors
ca. 1895

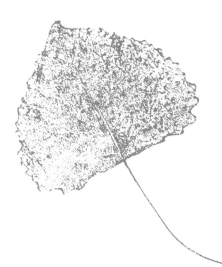

BE SURE TO...

◆ Identify the scratches or grooves on the rock at the mouth of the Lester River. These grooves were left by glaciers as they moved through the area about 14,000 years ago.

◆ Look for stands of aspen (poplar) along the shore from Lester River to Knife River.

◆ Stop at one of the many marked picnic wayside areas on the lake between Lester River and French River.

French River   7 miles

The Ojibwa named this river "Angwassago-zibi," or floodwood river.

The Minnesota Department of Natural Resources operates a modern cold-water fish hatchery here, incubating eggs from herring, sucker, and walleye, and rearing Atlantic salmon, chinook salmon, steelhead, and other strains of rainbow trout. Visitors are welcome 8 a.m. to 4 p.m. weekdays.

Which of these fish is native to the lake?

Herring
Suckers
Walleye
Atlantic Salmon
Chinook Salmon
Steelhead?

Answer on page 47.

Is this a trout or a salmon?

How you tell the difference ?
Answer on page 47.

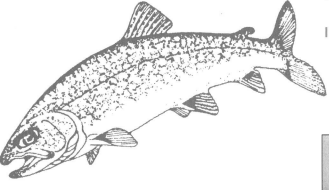

Copper was once found in the stream beds of this area. Rumors of large deposits of copper brought scores of prospectors to the North Shore in the 1840s and 1850s. From Lester River to Knife River, large amounts of money were spent in futile attempts to find copper deposits worth mining.

Buchanan   12.2 miles

Just over five miles northeast of French River, on the lake side of the road, a historic plaque commemorates this settlement. Platted in 1856, the townsite was named after President Buchanan and was the site of the North Shore's first post office. The first North Shore newspaper, The North Shore Advocate, is said to have been published here in 1857. Though townspeople had great hopes, copper mining never materialized here. The town was eventually abandoned and later destroyed by fire.

**Commercial fisherman on the
North Shore ca. 1940**

Knife River 15.5 miles

The name comes from the Ojibwa word "Makomani," which refers to sharp rocks in the river bed.

Knife River is one of the North Shore's most active sport fishing areas.

The first white settlers here in the 1880s were commercial fishermen. In 1898, a logging operation was built that remained an active business until 1919.

Until 1929, this area was also the scene of unsuccessful attempts to mine copper.

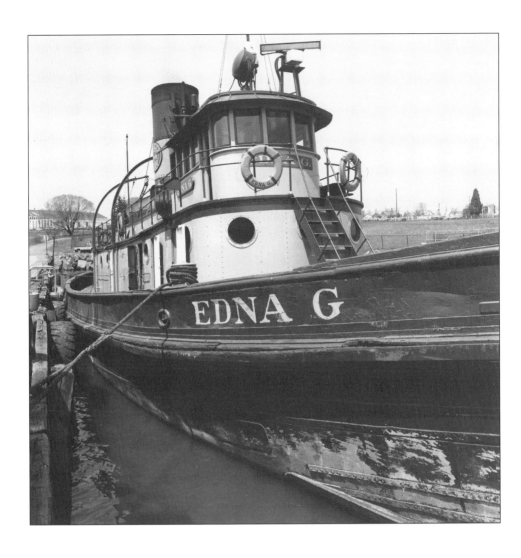

Two Harbors

The Edna G, the Great Lakes' first steam-powered tug, is now retired and docked at Agate Bay

Two Harbors   21.5 miles

Before 1856, the area around these two bays was well known Ojibwa hunting and fishing grounds.

In 1856, the village of Burlington was platted here and later named Agate Bay. In 1907, the village became the city of Two Harbors.

Originally, the town was a logging center. With the completion of the railway from the town of Tower located on Minnesota's iron range, Two Harbors became the state's first iron ore port in 1884. For years the iron ore industry was the basis of the town's economy. But, by the 1950s, all the high-grade iron ore had been taken from the ground. Iron ore is now mined as taconite, a low-grade iron-bearing rock that must be processed before it can be used to make steel.

BE SURE TO...

◆ Look for the house on the northwest corner of Second Avenue and Waterfront Drive. Now a museum operated by the Lake County Historical Society, this house was the original office of the Minnesota Mining and Manufacturing (3M) Company, which was organized in Two Harbors in 1902.

◆ Visit the Lake County Historical Museum located in the old depot of the Duluth, Mesabi and Iron Range (DM&IR) Railroad. The museum is on Agate Bay. Examine samples of local gemstones, agate and thomsonite in case you plan to look for these gemstones on the beaches of the North Shore.

◆ View the ore docks in Agate Bay from the observation platform at Paul VanHoven Park. Look for the Edna G, the Great Lakes' first steam powered tug. The Edna G, which was built in 1896, is now retired.

◆ Drive to the recently expanded boat launch parking area on Agate Bay, visit the lighthouse, and walk out onto the breakwall. Submerged west of the breakwall lies the Samuel P. Ely, a three-masted schooner. The Ely went down in 1896 and is one of the oldest recorded shipwrecks on Lake Superior. Try fishing for trout and salmon off the breakwall.

◆ See the Peter Toth Indian sculpture at the Visitor's Information Center. The sculpture was a gift to the people of Minnesota by the artist in tribute to Native Americans. Inside the information center, notice the large size of the logs used to construct this building.

◆ Explore the beach at Burlington Bay and test the temperature of Lake Superior's water.

◆ Look for Dock Number 1, located in Two Harbors' Agate Bay. It was once the largest iron ore loading dock in the world. Dock Number 1 is closest to the shore.

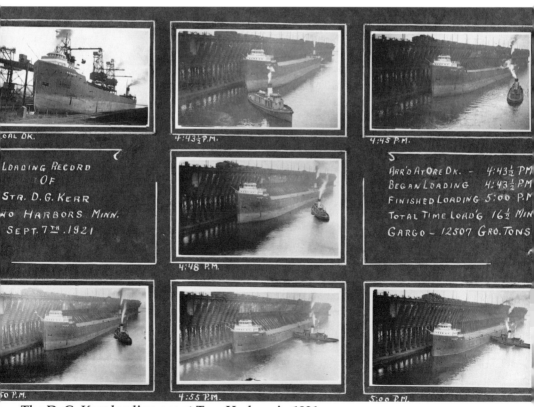

The D. G. Kerr loading ore at Two Harbors in 1921

Try This at Burlington Bay

Put both hands into the lake and open them wide.

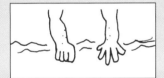

Clench one hand into a fist. After one minute, which hand seems warmer?

Now open your hand and move it through the water. Does your hand feel colder when it is moving or when it is still?

The average temperature of Lake Superior is 39°F, although the surface water temperature along the North Shore varies from about 40°F to about 65°F during the summer. No matter what time of year, the lake is cold.

Floating in 50° water, your body loses heat so fast, exhaustion or unconsciousness would probably occur in less than one hour. Death would occur within about three hours. Because exhaustion and loss of muscle control occur rapidly in cold water, personal flotation devices (life jackets) are essential to survival. A life jacket, which reduces body heat loss and provides support, gives you more than twice as much time to be rescued.

Based on your experiment, which of the following would be the best way to survive the longest possible time, assuming you are a long way from help?

A) Float quietly in a stretched out position.

B) Float quietly while curled up in a ball.

C) Swim and splash as vigorously as you can.

Answer

We certainly hope you never end up in such a situation, but if you do, remember answer "B" would best conserve body heat until help arrives. Swimming in cold water causes you to lose heat 35 percent faster than holding still.

Two Harbors to Castle Danger

Flood Bay   22.5 miles

This natural harbor offers a panoramic view of the lake and an opportunity to get close to the water on a Lake Superior pebble beach.

Silver Creek Cliff   26 miles

Silver Creek is the English translation for "Shonia-sibiwishe," the Ojibwa name for this area.

Four miles north of Two Harbors, the highway rises 125 feet above the lake. The bluff rises another 175 feet above the highway. A cut had to be blasted out of the rock of Silver Cliff in 1923 to make way for the North Shore's first road. Now, 70 years later, construction is underway to build a tunnel through the bluff.

Encampment River   28.5 miles

Immediately north of Silver Cliff is the Encampment forest, 1,500 acres of one of the last remaining stands of white and red pine along the North Shore. No one knows how or why these trees escaped the loggers' axes and saws. The forest is now privately owned.

?

Who loses body heat faster?

Children or adults?

Thin people or heavier people?

Optimists or pessimists?

Answers on page 47.

You will probably notice that most of the rocks on Lake Superior are flat. Why do you think there aren't more round rocks? It is probably because round rocks are more likely to be washed or rolled into the lake by the waves that frequently crash onto the beaches. This leaves the flatter rocks behind.

Most of the black rocks are basalt, the most common type of volcanic rock. Most of the reddish rocks are rhyolite, a less common volcanic rock that is a type of felsite lava. Although found all along the North Shore, the major outcroppings of rhyolite are found in the palisade area near the Baptism River and just north of Grand Marais.

What color are the rocks on the beaches? Do the rocks look different when they're wet?

Collect a sample of rocks and arrange them in line from the darkest to the lightest or from the most to the least reddish. Watch to see if the overall color of the rocks changes from one beach to another as you travel up the shore.

Build a big tower out of the flat rocks.

Try skipping the flat rocks on the lake.

?

How was Lake Superior formed?

Answer on page 47.

Lafayette Bluff 28.7 miles

The bluff and tunnel north of milepost 334 is named after a shipwreck. The iron ore freighter, Lafayette, sank here in 1905 in one of the most violent "N'oreaster" storms on record. During this three-day storm, the average wind velocity was 43 mph. The wind blew at a speed of 60-64 mph for 13 hours. This tragic storm emphasized the need for a lighthouse in the area.

How many ships have sunk in Lake Superior?

Answer on page 48.

Castle Danger 32 miles

Once a fishing and logging area, some say this site was named for its castle-like formation and because it was a dangerous area for ships. Others say it was named after the ship Castle, which sank here. No evidence of the ship has ever been found.

Lake Superior is a dangerous lake for ships because it is so unpredictable; storms develop suddenly and can create waves up to 30 feet high.

Castle Danger to Split Rock State Park

Gooseberry Falls State Park 35 miles

In Ojibwa, this river's name, "Shabonimikanizibe," means place of the gooseberries. The river got its name either for the gooseberry bushes growing wild along its banks or for Groseilliers, an early explorer of the area whose name in French means gooseberry bush.

Above the highway bridge are two waterfalls with a total drop of 30 feet. Below the bridge are two falls with a total drop of 75 feet. The park has more than 10 miles of foot trails. They wind upstream to a fifth falls, inland into forest areas and downstream to an agate beach at the mouth of the river.

Information on the history of the North Shore and excellent field guides to plants and trees, birds, fish and wildlife of the area are available at the park's interpretive center.

BE SURE TO...

◆ Check the bulletin board at the interpretive center for nature programs.

◆ Look for lava ledges from ancient flows and the four- and six-sided columns of lava rock near the upper and lower falls.

◆ Take the 1.5 mile self-guided Voyageur Nature Tour (leaflet available at the interpretive center), which winds upstream past the fifth falls and back through stands of aspen, cedar, and spruce.

◆ Follow the Lower Rim Trail down to the mouth of the river to picnic grounds and an agate beach.

Great Horned Owls are common on the North Shore and the surrounding forests.

About one billion years ago, a rupture in the earth's crust spewed forth layer upon layer of lava over this area. Some of these lava flows are visible today, especially near the waterfalls.

As the flows cooled, each at a different time, escaping gas bubbles rendered the top layer of each flow porous and therefore more susceptible to erosion. As the Gooseberry River found its way from high locations down to the lake, it washed away the porous portions of the lava flows, producing the rock ledges that can be seen by the falls today.

During the cooling periods, the lava also shrank, often breaking into four and six-sided columns. Water erosion has since left some of these angular columns exposed.

Gooseberry Falls

Try using the night sky as early navigators often did. Determining how far the North Star "Polaris" is from the northern horizon will give you a fairly accurate estimate of your latitude on Earth. This is true wherever you are in the northern hemisphere. Knowing the latitude was very important to early sailors as they tried to keep a steady course on the open seas.

Latitude is measured in degrees, north or south, from the equator; the equator is 0 degrees, the north pole is 90 degrees north, and the south pole is 90 degrees south.

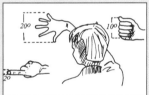

You can use your fingers and hands as tools for measuring objects in the night sky. A finger held at arm's length covers about two degrees of sky, a fist eight to ten degrees, and a spread hand about 20 degrees. (This technique generally works well for adults and children alike because their finger width to arm length is proportionally the same).

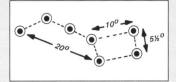

URSA MAJOR

1. Check your "measuring tools" using the Big Dipper. Our sky map shows the Big Dipper as part of the constellation Ursa Major.

2. Use the map to locate the North Star, Polaris, the star at the end of the Little Dipper's handle. Point to the North Star, then lower your arm to the horizon. You are pointing true north.

How many degrees is Polaris from the horizon? Figuring this out will give you a fairly accurate estimate of your latitude. (This technique works best with a level horizon).

What is your estimated latitude in degrees north? Gooseberry Falls State Park is 47 degrees north.

How close was your estimate? The latitude of Grand Portage is 48 degrees. Minneapolis and St. Paul are located 45 degrees north.

3. Measure the distances between some of the brightest stars you see.

Gooseberry State Park 47° N.

Using the night sky map, see if any of these bright stars are part of constellations.

4. Every 24 hours the earth makes one 360 degree rotation (like a spinning top). That means the earth turns 15 degrees every hour.

With these facts, you can use your fingers or hand to estimate the time remaining until sunset and moonset.

North Horizon Constellations
July-August

July 1 at 11:30p.m.
July 15 at 10:30p.m.
August 1 at 9:30p.m.
August 15 at 8:30p.m.

☆ North Star(Polaris)
● Stars
— Constellations

Cygnus
Draco
Cepheus
Little Dipper
Ursa Major
Big Dipper
Ursa Minor
Cassiopeia
Andromeda
Pegasus
Perseus

W   N   E

18

Split Rock State Park   38.5 miles

The park is called Split Rock because, when viewed from the water, one of the cliffs appears to be split in two.

In 1901, the Minnesota Abrasive Company began mining corundum west of the lighthouse. This site is now known as Corundum Point. Corundum, an extremely hard mineral, was in demand for grinding wheels. In 1903, the company was purchased by a new competitor in corundum mining, the Minnesota Mining and Manufacturing Company (3M). The company had been organized in Two Harbors the year before and had begun another corundum mining venture farther north near the Baptism River.

Splitrock Lighthouse lens.

Every night for nearly 60 years, the Split Rock lighthouse beamed a light across the lake in ten second intervals.

A few years later, after learning that the rock was anorthosite and not rare corundum, the 3M Company turned to manufacturing sand paper. Founded on a shoestring and a mistake, 3M is now one of the largest industrial companies in the world. Since 1910, its headquarters have been located in St. Paul.

Split Rock Lighthouse 40.5 miles

Iron ore mining in Minnesota was at its peak at the turn of the century. Fleets of freighters which were loaded with ore at the ports of Duluth and Two Harbors, traveled down the Great Lakes toward the steel mills in the East. During this time, the Sault Ste. Marie locks and canal system handled six times more shipping in eight months than the Panama Canal handled in one year.

The long recognized need for a lighthouse in this area was finally acknowledged in 1905 when the U.S. Government allocated funds. Construction began in May 1909.

Building a lighthouse at Split Rock was difficult because there was no road along the North Shore. When the first load of construction materials arrived by boat, a derrick had to be

Severe storms on the western arm of Lake Superior made a lighthouse important to ships' safety. There is another reason a lighthouse was needed. What is it?

Answer on page 48

In the late-season storms of 1905, 215 lives were lost and nearly 30 ships were damaged on Lake Superior.

erected near the top edge of the cliff and firmly anchored to the rock surface. Within a year, despite difficult conditions, 310 tons of building materials were hoisted up the 100-foot cliff from boats moored below. Construction was completed and the lighthouse went into operation on August 1, 1910.

Every night for nearly 60 years, the light shone out across the lake in ten-second intervals. The light had an official range of 22 miles, although it was identified by fishermen as far away as Grand Marais, more than 60 miles to the north.

The station was closed in 1969. Electronic navigational devices had made it obsolete. The Minnesota Historical Society now operates this historic site and gives tours on the history of the lighthouse and information on how the lens and light operated.

BE SURE TO...

◆ Stop at the wayside area on the lake side of the highway just southwest of the Split Rock River. Trails will take you to the mouth of the river and to several overlooks on the shore. This is also an access point to the Superior Hiking Trail.

◆ Visit Split Rock Lighthouse.

◆ Climb to the top of the lighthouse to see the lens that still floats in 250 pounds of mercury.

◆ Tour the keeper's house which has been restored to its pre-1930s condition.

◆ Take the trail to the southeast that leads down to the rocky shore for a good view of the lighthouse 125 feet above the lake.

Nature trails at Split Rock are accessible and easy for young children.

Split Rock State Park
Junction Hwy. 1

Beaver Bay 45 miles

Founded by German immigrants in 1856, Beaver Bay is the oldest continuous settlement on Minnesota's Superior shore. The German founders opened the region's first sawmill, providing employment for most of the townspeople. The sawmill also employed many Ojibwa. Beaver Bay became known for friendly relations between the immigrant settlers and the Ojibwa.

German immigrants settled here in 1856, but other cultures lived here for thousands of years before they arrived. Who were the first inhabitants of the shore?

Answer on pages 48-49.

Ojibwa family ca. 1900

Logging camp, 1915

The Reserve Mining Company's taconite processing plant near Silver Bay, 1959

A totem pole on the upper side of the first street away from the lake marks an Indian cemetery containing burial plots from 1865.

Silver Bay   49 miles

Silver Bay was founded in 1956 by the Reserve Mining Company to house the workers at its newly built, and first of its kind, taconite processing plant. The plant was built here on the shore because of its need for large amounts of water. It is the only taconite plant not built at a mining site. At full capacity, the plant could produce more than nine million tons of iron ore pellets per year.

Until 1974, 67,000 tons of waste rock, called tailings, were dumped into the lake every day. When public concern over water quality ended in a court dispute, Reserve Mining agreed to dump the tailings on land several miles from shore.

BE SURE TO...

◆ Look for the totem pole that marks the Indian cemetery and the bronze plaque that names the Indians buried there. John Beargrease is also buried in this cemetery. He became a North Shore legend, making the 125-mile trip between Two Harbors and Grand Portage every week to deliver the mail. In winter, he used a dog sled. The John Beargrease dog sled race, held each winter, follows his old route.

Palisade Head 52 miles

Here begins the dense reddish lava formation
known as the palisades. For the next 40 miles as
you travel northward, you will see a rugged
and forested coastline.

The turn-off to the Palisade overlook is at
milepost 357 on the lake side of the highway.
Enjoy the view from Palisade Head, 348 feet
above the water, and look for Shovel Point, two
miles to the north.

Legends say that Indians would test their
archery skills by attempting to shoot arrows
from canoes on the lake to the top of Palisade
Head.

**Netting fish at the mouth
of the Baptism River, 1910.**

Baptism River, Tettegouche State Park 53.5 miles

Because French missionaries used these waters to baptize new converts, the name Au Bapteme was given to the river. Once called Baptism River State Park, this area is now part of the larger Tettegouche State Park. There is a large rest area and information center at the Baptism wayside.

The name "Tettegouche," meaning retreat, was given to this area by the Micmac tribe. These Indians were brought here from the East Coast by the first lumbermen of the area to work in the logging camps.

Between milepost 358 and 359 on the lake side of the highway, is a turn-off to two parking areas. Well-marked trails from the lower parking lot lead to the mouth of the Baptism River and upstream more than a mile to the nearly 80-foot High Falls. From the upper parking lot, the three-quarter mile Shovel Point Trail leads toward the lake for almost a quarter of a mile, and then turns left. This trail offers a gorgeous hike to the end of Shovel Point, a wonderful place to view the palisade shoreline.

Name at least two industries that provided jobs for the people of the North Shore.

Answer on page 49.

BE SURE TO...

◆   Drive the narrow, winding road to the Palisade Head overlook for a breathtaking view of the area. Do your exploring carefully.

◆   Take the trail to Shovel Point (allow an hour for the round trip) and the trails to both the mouth of the Baptism River and upstream to the High Falls. The hike to the High Falls takes about 45 minutes each way.

◆   Look for rock climbers on the faces of the nearly vertical cliffs along the palisades.

Today's John Beargrease dog sled race follows the same 125-mile route from Two Harbors to Grand Portage.

Try This at Baptism River

Remember the old saying: "When in nature take only photographs, leave only footprints." So, instead of collecting, check off the things you see and give yourself a score.

(5 pts)_____1. A fuzzy leaf

(5 pts)_____2. A spider web

(5 pts)_____3. A rotting log

(5 pts)_____4. A bird feather

(5 pts)_____5. A plant growing on a rock

(5 pts)_____6. A ship on the lake

(5 pts)_____7. A sandbar at the mouth of a river

(5 pts)_____8. An orange-colored mushroom (fungus)

(5 pts)_____9. A tree over 30 feet tall

(5 pts)_____ 10. A hole in the tree made by an animal

(5 pts)_____ 11. A hole in the ground made by an animal

(10 pts)_____12. A chipmunk

(10 pts)_____13. A piece of colored glass worn smooth on a beach

(10 pts)_____14. Two kinds of ever- green trees

(15 pts)_____15. Three kinds of wildflowers

BONUS FINDS (20 pts each):

_____A rainbow near a waterfall

_____Moonrise over the lake (or the northern lights)

_____An agate, Minnesota's state rock, or thomsonite

_____Animal tracks

SCORING:

80-100 Super naturalists

60-80 Pretty good naturalists

40-60 Good observers

20-40 Keep looking

Junction Hwy. 1 to Schroeder

Junction Hwy. 1, Crosby-Manitou State Park   55 miles

County Road 7 is the entrance to George Crosby-Manitou State Park, a large undeveloped park established for hikers and backpacking campers.

Little Marais   59 miles

Meaning "little marsh" in French, Little Marais was once an active logging area and a place where logs were collected in rafts and towed along the North Shore to Duluth.

Manitou River   63 miles

The name comes from the Ojibwa word "Manitou," which means Great Spirit. The river begins by winding through George Crosby-Manitou State Park. Then the river flows through a deep gorge and plunges into Lake Superior, forming the only falls with a straight drop into the lake. The falls are on privately owned land.

Caribou River   66 miles

This wayside rest area is a nice place for a picnic. Unless the river is extremely high, it is also a safe place for children to explore a North Shore stream.

The river gets its name from woodland caribou, a type of deer closely related to reindeer that were abundant in these forests about 100 years ago. Today, they are found mostly in Canada.

The stands of large birch trees from here to Schroeder are evidence that much of this area was burned in the forest fire of 1926.

Just past the Caribou River is the Cook County line. Minnesota's Cook County is named after Major Michael Cook, a civil war hero from Faribault, Minnesota, who died in battle in Nashville, Tennessee, in 1864.

There are four kinds of trout in Lake Superior and its tributaries. Which one is this?

Answer on pages 50-52.

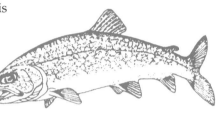

Why are caribou no longer found in Minnesota?

Answer on page 52.

Fishing a stream is different from fishing the quiet water of a lake. Successful stream fishing depends a great deal on knowing how to "read" the moving water to discover where fish would feed and where they would rest.

At the Caribou River, collect a handful of small sticks. Check the river's speed (velocity) by marking a point on the bank and pacing a distance up the river (about 20 feet). Throw a stick into the river and see how long it takes for the stick to reach the mark.

Can you find an area that is slower? Slow stretches of the river allow fish to use less energy to remain in one place.

Rocky outcroppings, logs, waterfalls, and boulders may create unusual currents in the river. These changes in the river's flow may offer fish a place to feed or rest.

Can you find an area of river where the water turns and appears to flow upstream? This is called an "eddy."

Throw a stick just behind (downstream) a boulder that is in the middle of the river. Is the water immediately behind the boulder moving as fast as the water flowing beside the boulder? What happens farther back from the boulder?

If you can safely reach an area near the base of the waterfalls, try throwing a stick near the falls. Does the stick float downstream or do recirculating currents draw it back upstream to the falls?

Riffles, eddies and turbulent areas are where the native brook trout or planted brown and rainbow trout may be found feeding. The quiet waters behind rocks and logs or the water in deep pools more likely hold trout that are resting or seeking shade from the midsummer sun.

Taconite Harbor   72 miles

Recorded on earlier maps as Two Island River, this area is now the site of a power plant that supplies the LTV Mining Company's Iron Range taconite plants with electricity. This is also a shipping site, and you may observe taconite being loaded onto ships.

Schroeder   75 miles

The town gets its name from the Schroeder Lumber Company, which operated here on the Cross River around the turn of the century and employed nearly 1,000 men.

During a fierce storm in 1846, the mouth of this river provided safe refuge for Father Frederick Baraga, a missionary priest, as he traveled by canoe across the lake from the Wisconsin shore to minister to the Indians. In gratitude for his safe landing, the Indians erected a crude wooden cross at the river's mouth and named the river "Tchibaiatogo-zibi", or spirit of the soul river. A permanent cross has since been erected at this site.

Affectionately called the "snowshoe priest," Father Baraga came to America from Yugoslavia in 1830 and traveled all over this region. In addition to his duties as a priest, Father Baraga translated the Bible into Ojibwa and wrote the first Ojibwa grammar book and dictionary.

BE SURE TO...

◆ Take an inland loop trip to view the hills and get a ridgetop view of Lake Superior. One suggestion is to take State Highway 1 to Finland (an early Finnish logging settlement). Crosby Manitou state park has beautiful vistas of the lake, accessible by rugged hiking trails. Return to Little Marais on the shore via County Road 6.

◆ Stop at the Caribou River wayside rest area for a picnic and explore a North Shore stream. Hike to Caribou Falls, one-half mile upstream.

◆ Stop in the town of Schroeder and view the Cross River Falls from the highway bridge.

Monument to Fr. Baraga at Schroeder

Schroeder to Lutsen

Temperance River
State Park   77 miles

The Ojibwa named this place "Kawinbash," meaning deep hollow. The river falls rapidly (160 feet in one-half mile) before emptying into Lake Superior. The swirling action of the water has been carving potholes into the rock for centuries.

After Europeans settled the area, the river was humorously named for the fact that it was the only river with no "bar" (sandbar) at its mouth. A sand bar is formed by lake waves pushing sand up against the shore. The force of a fast-moving river may prevent sand from building up. Occasionally, this river doesn't live up to its name and a sandbar will form. Do you see one?

This park has many miles of hiking trails that lead along the river gorge and into the Superior National Forest. The park entrance is just northeast of the river. There is a wayside rest and parking area at the Temperance River.

Tofte   78 miles

Founded by Norwegian immigrants in 1898, this town was once a logging and commercial fishing settlement and an important boat landing.

The Sawbill Trail (Cook County Hwy. 2), which leads to inland lakes, canoe routes, and camping grounds of the Boundary Waters Canoe Area Wilderness (BWCAW), begins here.

Two miles west of Tofte is Carlton Peak, one of the highest points along the North Shore with an elevation of 927 feet above lake level and 1527 feet above sea level. It is quite a scramble to the top, but the view is worth it.

BE SURE TO...

◆   Hike the many trails in Temperance River State Park and look for the circular formations made by the falls in the lava rock. Keep children in hand.

◆   Climb to the top of Carlton Peak for a terrific view of the lake and surrounding area. To get there, drive 2.5 miles up the Sawbill Trail to the sanitary landfill. Turn left onto a dirt road, which may be rough. At the end of the road, an unmarked trail takes you to the 250-foot uphill climb.

◆   Take the Leveaux and Oberg Mountain Trails. Both trails begin from a parking lot approximately two miles inland. Take the first left-hand turn after the Onion River (Forest Road 336) just north of the Ray Bergland State Wayside between Lutsen and Tofte. The gravel road turnoff is marked "Superior Hiking Trail" on the lake side of Highway 61.

The Leveaux Mountain Trail is a 1.5 mile loop which winds through maple stands, a colorful hike in the fall.

The Oberg Mountain trail is a 1.5 mile loop that provides views of Lake Superior, bluffs and ridges. It is a self-guided wildflower identification walk. Brochures may be available at the trail head.

Temperance River

?

What causes the water of some North Shore streams to take on the color of root beer?

Answer on page 52.

31

As you hike into the north woods, imagine the land as it must have appeared 200 years ago when most of Minnesota was covered with pine forest. White pine, the logger's prize, were often five to six feet in diameter and up to 200 feet high. Minnesota's state tree, the red pine, grew to three feet in diameter and reached 100 feet in height. All of the giant pines were felled by the loggers. You may still see a few white and red pine growing along the North Shore, but these pines are not old enough to be more than two feet in diameter and 50 to 70 feet in height.

White Pine

Red Pine

What are the largest trees you see along the North Shore? What is their height and their diameter? An easy method of measuring the height of a tree requires a short stick and the help of a friend. Hold the stick vertically at arm's length and position yourself so that the top and bottom of the tree appears the same height as the stick. Keep your arm extended and turn the stick horizontally. Ask a family member or friend to start from the base of the tree and walk at a right angle to you. Stop the person when he or she appears to reach the end of the stick (see illustrations). The distance between the person and the tree should equal the height of the tree.

Pace this distance to find the height of the tree.

At Temperance River, take the Cauldron Trail on the east side of the river (a short way above the highway) to an open area where the river takes a bend and you can see the water falling through the dark and narrow rock canyon. Try to measure the height of the double-trunked cedar tree on the east bank that leans toward the river and seems to be clinging to the rock with its exposed root system.

One method of estimating the diameter of a tree is to hug it. A person's arm span (finger tip to finger tip) is approximately equal to his or her height. If the ratio of diameter to circumference is about one to three (actually about 3.14), then a person with a six foot arm span should be able to hug a tree almost two feet in diameter with his or her finger tips just touching.

A giant pine five to six feet in diameter would have a circumference of 16 to 18 feet. How many of you does it take to make a circle that big?

Find a tree to hug that is just your arm span and figure its diameter.

Arm span (or height) (feet)	Approximate diameter of tree (inches)
3	11.5
4	15
4.5	17
5	19
5.5	21
6	23

Lutsen to Grand Marais

Lutsen 85 miles

The name comes from a 1632 battle site in Germany in which the Swedish King Gustavus Adolphus was killed.

An important logging center at the turn of the century, the Lutsen area is also the site of one of the first resorts on the North Shore and in the state. This area is now a year-round recreational area with resorts, trails, skiing, snowmobiling, and hiking.

The Caribou Trail (Cook County Hwy. 4) begins here and ends at Brule Lake.

Cascade River State Park 95.2 miles

The Cascade River and nine other streams flow through this park on their way to the lake. With many lakes and swamps at its headwaters, the Cascade River is an excellent trout stream.

How are the potholes formed in the lava rock near water falls?

Answer on page 52.

The North Shore has hundreds of miles of excellent hiking trails.

These plants are common to the cool moist soil of the north woods. Can you find all of them?

Remember that early summer (before mid-July) is best for finding wild flowers, and late summer (after mid-July) is best for finding wild fruits and berries.

Thimbleberry (or Flowering Raspberry)

In Minnesota, this plant is found only in the northeast region of the state and it is abundant along the North Shore. The plant is in the rose family and grows two to four feet high. The large leaves are wide and lobed, much like a maple leaf. In the early summer, the plant displays showy white flowers about two inches across and, in late summer, flat orange-red, raspberry-like berries. Although quite tasteless, the berries are edible and make excellent jam or jelly.

Bunchberry (or Dwarf Cornel)

This low-growing ground cover is a member of the dogwood family. (Its flower resembles that of the flowering dogwood shrub.) Look for patches of these very symmetrical plants showing one-inch wide white flowers in early summer and bunches of red berries in late summer. Indians were said to mix these berries with other ingredients to make a pudding.

Bracken Fern

Ferns are non-flowering plants that grow throughout the world. The bracken fern is the most common. The leaves of the bracken fern are distinctively triangular and fan out almost horizontally from the center of the plant. Look for knee-high colonies of this dark green fern in the north woods. New growth is coiled up in structures called fiddleheads, named because they resemble the scroll at the end of a violin.

Canada Mayflower (or False Lily of the Valley)

This low-growing plant is in the lily family. Each plant has two to three shiny, broad-pointed leaves that are heart shaped at their base. In early summer, you will find small white flowers in upright clusters and, in late summer, very small green-speckled berries.

Clintonia Lily (or Blue-bead Lily)

This plant, also in the lily family, grows to less than one foot in height and has a clump of three to five shiny, elliptical leaves. Ojibwa women used these berries to create artistic designs in their handwork by biting into the leaf blades. Pale yellow, lily-like flowers three-fourths of an inch long appear on a tall stem in early summer. In late summer, the plant shows large blue berries. *These berries are poisonous.*

To learn more about the wild flowers of northern Minnesota, pick up the brochure on the wild flowers of the Oberg Trail. This self-guided tour is a joint effort of the Lutsen-Tofte Garden Club and the Forest Service. Brochures are available at the trail site or the Forest Service Ranger Station in Tofte.

An extensive and well-groomed trail system on both sides of this picturesque river begins from a wayside parking area on the highway one-half mile southwest of the park entrance. Upstream are the spectacular upper falls. As the river flows its last three miles to Lake Superior, it drops 900 feet over a series of magnificent steps. These lower falls give the river its name. Be sure to take the Cascade River Trail to a spot where five waterfalls can be seen at one time. The Lookout Mountain Trail, which branches off the Cascade River Trail, makes for a great hike in any season, and leads to an overlook of the lake and surrounding area.

In winter, the Cascade area is the site of one of the largest deer yards in the state, with a density often reaching 100 deer per square mile.

Thomsonite Beach   97 miles

A two-mile stretch of shore between mileposts 402 and 404 is one of the few places in the world where thomsonite, a semi-precious gemstone, is found. This land is privately owned.

Formed by mineral deposits in the gas bubbles of the lava flows, thomsonite can vary in quality, color, and pattern. The only semi-precious thomsonite in the country is found here on this short stretch of shore. It is only here that the unique green and pink-eye patterned thomsonite is found.

Why do deer congregate along the shore in winter?

Answer on page 52.

Good Harbor Bay   99 miles

At milepost 404 a small wayside area above this bay provides a good view of the lake. An historic marker points out that the highway cut has exposed one of the few North Shore sandstone beds. The bed is overlaid with lava.

Look for thomsonite washed up at nearby Cut Face Creek on the north side of the bay.

Look for the layer of sandstone sandwiched between lava flows in the highway cut as you drive the curve around Good Harbor Bay. Check for thomsonite at Cut Face Creek.

Grand Marais

Grand Marais   105 miles

The Indians called this area "Kitchibitobig," meaning double bay. The French named the area "Grand Marais," which means big marsh.

Try to visualize this natural harbor as it must have looked two hundred years ago. The area where the Coast Guard Station is located was once an island separated from the shore by a shallow marsh.

The city was founded in the early 1800s. The first white settlers arrived by boat. For a short time, Grand Marais was the site of a fur trading post. Later, commercial fishing and logging became more important. Harvesting wood is still a key industry, and piles of pulpwood can be seen along the shore of the man-made peninsula that now divides the bay. Grand Marais is the starting point for the famous 58-mile Gunflint Trail. The Gunflint Trail leads into the heart of the Superior National Forest and ends at Lake Saganaga, a Canadian border lake.

Grand Marais was once a major commercial fishing area. Like other communities along the lake it supported a thriving commercial fishery for decades until the lake's fishery began to decline.

Today, the fish population of Lake Superior is only a fraction of what it once was. Why?

See page 53 for answers.

Children can get a close look at gulls in Grand Marais and other beachfronts along the North Shore.   See descriptions of different gulls on page 38.

BE SURE TO...

◆   Visit the Cook County Historical Museum.

◆   Walk past the Coast Guard Station and out on the breakwater. If you look carefully, you may find initials and dates carved in the rocks by some of the first settlers. Be cautious of the waves when out on the breakwater! View the city from the breakwater, and look for the Sawtooth Mountains rising behind the city.

◆   Explore the peninsula northeast of the lighthouse. Notice that the common plants are different on either side of the peninsula. This is due to the strength of the wind on the lake side as compared with the bay side.

◆   View the lake and surrounding area from the Gunflint Trail overlook.

◆   Look for the historic landmark, the St. Francis Xavier Church, located just northeast of town at the old Indian settlement of Chippewa City. The now abandoned church is significant for its French architecture.

The two most common seagulls along the North Shore are very similar in appearance. Both the adult Herring Gull and the adult Ring-billed Gull have white heads, greyish wings with black and white tips and white bellies. There are two obvious differences: The Herring Gull has a red spot near the tip of its lower bill and pink or flesh-colored legs. The Ring-billed Gull has a dark ring around its bill near the tip and green-yellow legs. One- and two-year-old gulls of both types are similar to adults in size and shape but have darker feathers.

Just as people understand the intention of somebody shaking a fist at them, gulls and other birds have body postures and behaviors that tell their fellow gulls how they feel and what they intend to do.

Threatening or aggressive behavior is shown when gulls have their wings held slightly out from their bodies or part of their wings are cocked forward ready to use in beating another bird.

Birds that have slightly raised wings and are walking toward another in either an upright fashion with their bill pointing down and ready to strike, or with their body in a forward position, are particularly threatening.

Try to find a "bossy" gull, one that is showing a threatening or aggressive posture.

Identify "intimidated" or "anxious" gulls. Gulls that are not willing to stand their ground when intimidated hold their wings flush against their sides unless they are beginning to fly away. Frequently, they will have an upright posture, but their bills will be pointed horizontally or upward.

Identify a "submissive" bird. In this position, gulls have their wings flush against their sides, backs hunched, and necks withdrawn. The posture is most commonly seen with young gulls or females that are near their mates.

Can you identify other postures or behaviors that seem to convey a message to other gulls? What do you think they mean?

Grand Marais to Pigeon River
(Canadian Border)

Kadunce (or Kodonce) Creek
113.5 miles

The stream was named by early settlers who drank its high mineral content water. The name in French means diarrhea. Its reputation has improved over the years and is now a popular trout fishing stream.

Judge Magney State Park   119 miles

This is the last park before the Canadian border. It is a prime camping and hiking area.

The park is named in honor of Clarence R. Magney, former mayor of Duluth and justice of the Minnesota Supreme Court. Judge Magney devoted a great deal of time, energy, and money to protect much of the land along the North Shore.

The Brule River, with its beginnings at Brule Lake, flows through this scenic park. The river provides a challenge to both trout fishing and white-water canoeing enthusiasts. Three miles of scenic trails wind through the park to several waterfalls, including Pothole Falls, where the river disappears into the mysterious "Devil's Cauldron."

?

Why, in summer, do rivers in the southern part of the North Shore, such as the Gooseberry and Baptism Rivers, run more slowly than those in the northern part?

Answer on page 53.

Hovland   123 miles

Founded by Norwegian immigrants, this area was once an active log rafting and commercial fishing site. The old cement dock can still be seen.

The Arrowhead Trail (Cook County Hwy. 16) begins here and leads to the BWCA (Boundary Waters Canoe Area)

Reservation River   129 miles

Although it once had the Indian name "Mesqua-Tawangewi-zibi," meaning red sand river, the river now gets its name from the fact that it is the western boundary of the reservation lands of the Grand Portage Band of Ojibwa Indians. It is one of the few North Shore streams that decends gradually from its source and does not cascade over waterfalls.

BE SURE TO...

◆   Hike the well-marked trails upstream on the east side of the river in Judge Magney State Park that will take you to the mysterious "Devil's Cauldron." Where do you think the water goes? The falls are found 1 to 1.5 miles from the highway.

Kids can find a variety of birds along the shore. See page 42 for descriptions of common species.

Several North Shore rivers offer excellent fly fishing.

BE SURE TO...

◆ Try your trout fishing skills at either Kimball or Kadunce Creeks.

◆ Explore Paradise Beach located 4.5 miles northeast of Kadunce Creek.

◆ Notice how the terrain changes as you drive north from Grand Marais. One of the most spectacular parts of Minnesota is the area between Grand Portage and the Pigeon River. These hills and ridges are formed of a slate-like bedrock that is highly resistant to erosion.

What kinds of birds have you seen on your North Shore trip? You are almost certain to see gulls, ravens, crows, a few ducks, maybe a loon, and possibly a hawk or two.

Raven

Crow

Gull

Gulls, ravens, and crows are part of nature's clean-up crew who scavenge for discarded food and also feed on dead animals. Gulls flock wherever food is available, especially around garbage dumps and commercial fishing operations. You will often see ravens and crows feeding on animals that have been killed on the road. Ravens are only found in Minnesota around the North Shore area. Can you tell the difference between a raven and a crow?

On the water, you may see mergansers and perhaps loons, both of which are fish-eating waterfowl that swim underwater to catch their food. Mallards can often be seen near shore during the summer months. Mallards prefer to eat insects, seeds, and plants and can be seen nibbling at the surface or feeding bottom-up in shallow water. They rarely dive completely under the surface.

Hawks and gulls use their long wings to soar the updrafts that are created along the shore. Lake Superior has a funneling effect on the fall migration of hawks and other birds of prey. Migrating hawks can be seen all along the shore but the best flyway site is at the western end of the lake at Hawk Ridge in Duluth. Hawk-watching begins in mid-August and continues into December with the biggest flights taking place around

Long tailed Hawk

Broad wing Hawk

Falcon

September 8-23. The best hawk-watching occurs on a clear day when the wind blows from the northwest. Fourteen species of birds of prey, including broad-winged hawks, sharp-shinned hawks, marsh hawks, red-tailed hawks, turkey vultures, bald eagles, and osprey are regular migrators over the Duluth flyway.

Mallard

Meganser

Loon

Grand Portage

Grand Portage 135 miles

The city is located on the Grand Portage Ojibwa Indian Reservation which was created by the signing of the Treaty of LaPointe in 1854. The treaty, which predated Minnesota's statehood (1858), was between the U.S. government and the Ojibwa Indian nation.

The Ojibwa originally lived on the shores of the Atlantic Ocean, but, according to their oral tradition, migrated westward along the Great Lakes in search of the forest, streams, and the "food growing out of the water:" wild rice.

Both the Ojibwa and the Dakota (Sioux), who lived in this area before the Ojibwa, were familiar with the nine-mile portage around Pigeon River's High Falls that the French would later name "Grand Portage," meaning the great carrying place.

French explorers and the French Voyageurs were the first Europeans to visit the area, arriving in the 1600s. Fur trappers and merchants followed in pursuit of the beaver, whose pelt was used to make top hats. The Pigeon River was an important link in the waterway routes used by the fur traders as they journeyed between Montreal and the Northwest Territories.

During the 1700s, Grand Portage became the meeting place for Indians, trappers, and merchants. In 1778, England's Northwest Company built a trading post here, and it

BE SURE TO...

◆ Visit Grand Portage during the second weekend in August when Rendezvous Days are celebrated commemorating the great rendezvous of trappers and traders during the 1700s.

◆ Walk the one-half mile trail behind the monument up to Mt. Rose for a good view of the fort and Grand Portage Bay, as well as its neighbor, Wauswaugoning Bay. These are the largest bays on Minnesota's shore of Lake Superior

An Ojibwa community at Grand Portage painted in 1857 by Eastman Johnson

became the hub of North American fur trade. For a brief period in history, from 1778 to 1805, the Grand Portage area was the center of international trading activities. In 1805, the post was moved north to Fort William, Canada in order to avoid taxation by the American government.

A Sioux pow-wow.

Pigeon River   147 miles

Located six miles beyond Grand Portage, this river marks the border between the United States and Canada. The name comes from the translation of the Ojibwa name "Omimizibi," which refers to the large numbers of wild pigeons that once lived here.

The High Falls of the Pigeon River were impassable for the Voyageurs and the "grand portage" was used to gain access to the waters and land that lay to the northwest. High Falls can only be viewed by crossing into Canada and paying a fee to enter privately owned land. Just south of the border, there is an outstanding new wayside rest area.

Who were the voyageurs?

Answer on pages 53-54.

Pigeon River High Falls

BE SURE TO...

◆ Take the trail to Mt. Josephine to a point high on Superior's shore where you can see the Suzie Islands, three miles to the east in Wauswaugoning Bay.

◆ Take the boat trip to Isle Royale, 22 miles from shore. Grand Portage is the closest point to this island national park, which is part of Michigan.

◆ Follow in the historic footsteps of the Indians and fur traders and hike the arduous nine-mile Grand Portage Trail that ends at Fort Charlotte on the Pigeon River.

◆ Hike to the famous witch's tree on Hat Point.

◆ View the area from Wauswaugoning Bay overlook, just north of Grand Portage Bay.

The Ojibwa Indians had a system for writing messages using symbols familiar to all of the tribe. Messages were usually drawn with charcoal on birch bark or a flat piece of cedar and left by travelers for those who followed.

Below is a message that reads: "Two canoes stopped here together. One canoe camped two nights and had plenty of food. The other canoe stayed only one night, found no food, and left.

 -tipi

-how many nights were spent in tipi

 -fire with many bones, indicating good hunting and much food

-canoe

 -marks are for the number of children in the family

The animal symbols in the canoes represent both the father's family and the mother's family. Each family clan, or totem, had an animal symbol. There were about 20 original Ojibwa totems.

Actual pictograph from Superior National Forest.

Shown in the canoes are members of the Eagle: Catfish:

Caribou: and Bear totems

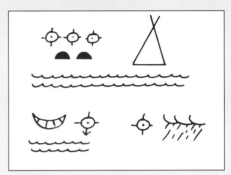

Now try decoding this message. Answer found below.

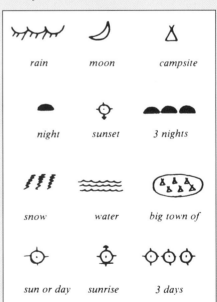

Here are some more Ojibwa symbols. Make up some symbols with your own meanings and write a message to a member of your family or a friend.

rain	moon	campsite
night	sunset	3 nights
snow	water	big town of
sun or day	sunrise	3 days

Answer: The message says: "We stayed at a campsite near water for three days and two nights. One evening we canoed on the water at sunset. One day it rained."

Questions and Answers

Is Lake Superior as polluted as the other Great Lakes?

No. Lake Superior's shores are not as developed with cities and industries as the other Great Lakes are. Consequently, the lake has never suffered as much pollution. However, this type of pollution is only a part of the story. All the Great Lakes suffer pollution from the atmosphere. Pollution falls onto the lake through rain, snow, and dry particles. Almost all the toxic pollution of Lake Superior (mercury, PCBs, persistent contaminants) comes from the atmosphere.

Which of these fish is native to Lake Superior?

Herring, suckers, and walleye are all native to Lake Superior. Atlantic salmon have been regularly stocked in the upper Great Lakes for more than one hundred years, but have not established breeding populations. Chinook salmon were stocked in Lake Michigan in 1873, but failed to establish permanent stocks. In 1967, Michigan again stocked Chinook salmon, this time to control alewife populations and to supplement stocks of the popular coho salmon. Chinook salmon reproduce and grow well in Lake Superior, but because they face stiff competition from other predator fish species for a limited number of forage fish, the chinook's future as part of the Great Lake fishery is uncertain. Steelhead, or rainbow trout, were planted in the Great Lakes a century ago. Lake Superior has many fine spawning streams for this popular game fish.

Is it a trout or a salmon?

The fish on the top is a trout; the one on the bottom is a salmon. It can be tough to tell these apart. The shape of the fish's tail, body markings, and the number of scales on the fish can all help you tell what kind of fish it is. The clearest differences: Pacific salmon have a black mouth and 13 or more anal fin rays. The trout has a white mouth and 12 or fewer anal fin rays.

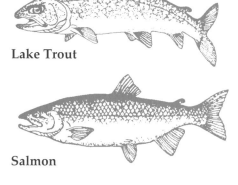

Lake Trout

Salmon

Who loses body heat faster?

Everyone reacts differently to the cold, even under the same conditions. Generally, children lose body heat more quickly than adults. Thin people lose body heat faster than heavy people, although recent research shows that some very fit athletes can maintain their body heat for a long time, even if they are very thin.

Anecdotal evidence suggests that a positive attitude helps people survive longer in cold water.

How was Lake Superior formed?

About one billion years ago intense volcanic activity began in this area and lasted for a period of 20 million years. During that time lava flowed over the area hundreds of times, accumulating to a thickness of nearly 3,000 feet. The volcanic activity, related to a deep fracture that extended from northeast Oklahoma to Lake Superior, nearly split North America apart. A similar fracture developed between Europe and North America about 100 million years ago and did split these two land masses, forming the Atlantic Ocean floor. In the Lake Superior region, the fracture stabilized, pressure from inside the earth convulsed the earth's surface and pushed the rock blanket upward. The rock rose slowly, subsided, and eventually tilted toward the area that would later become the Lake Superior basin.

Then, about one million years ago, the first of four ice ages took place. Throughout the ice ages, glaciers (sheets of ice thousands of feet thick) covered all of northern Minnesota and much of Canada. As these glaciers inched southward they scraped the earth, flattening mountains, pushing boulders, and carving out craters. These same glaciers gouged out the Lake Superior basin. The weight of the glaciers also depressed the land surrounding the basin.

About 11,000 years ago as the last glacier melted and receded northward at a rate of three city blocks per year, it formed an ice dam and created the ancient lake called Glacial Lake Duluth. The shoreline of this ancient lake was more than 500 feet above its present level.

With the removal of the thick glacial ice, the land along the shore (long depressed by the glacier's weight) began to rise to its pre-ice level. In fact, 90 percent of Superior's shoreline is characterized by bluffs formed during this uplift. The shore is still rebounding at a rate of a few feet per century.

As the melting glaciers uncovered outlets for the water, the lake level lowered in several steps until it reached its present level.

How many ships have sunk in Lake Superior?

More than 300 ships have sunk in the lake. At least 10 shipwrecks are accessible to SCUBA divers along the North Shore. For a list of wrecks and how to get to them, see resource list on p. 55.

Severe storms on the western arm of Lake Superior made a lighthouse important to ships' safety. There is another reason a lighthouse was needed. What is it?

The magnetic properties of the iron deposits in the area and the magnetic properties of ship's cargo disturbed compass readings and sent ships off-course toward the rocky shore.

German immigrants settled here in 1856, but other cultures lived here for thousands of years before they arrived. Who were the first inhabitants of the North Shore?

At the time the first European explorers (Pierre Radisson and Sieur des Groseillier) reached this area in the mid-1600s, the Dakota and Ojibwa Indians were in battle over the territory covering the western side of Lake Superior. The area, now known as Fond du Lac, had long been the territory of the Dakota Indian nation (Sioux). The conflict between the Dakota and Ojibwa (Chippewa) continued for about 140 years, into the 1800s. This conflict, together with the diminished migration of the buffalo into the Minnesota Territory, moved the Dakota westward to the plains.

With the exception of a few fur trading posts, the North Shore remained unoccupied by European

Settlers until the 1830s and the arrival of missionaries. It wasn't until 1854, however, when the Treaty of LaPointe was signed by the U.S. government and the Ojibwa nation, that European immigrants began to build permanent settlements along the North Shore.

Name at least two industries that have provided jobs for the people of the North Shore.

Four industries have provided the most jobs. Logging and mining were the earliest. Commercial fishing followed as many Scandinavian immigrants settled along the coast. Today tourism is one of the biggest employers.

LOGGING:

In the mid-1800s, rumors of copper and gold deposits attracted many hopeful prospectors to the North Shore. When only small amounts of these minerals were found, attention turned to the area's vast timber resources. The North Shore lumber era began in the 1850s, and for the next half century, lumber speculators became some of the wealthiest men in the country.

Those 50 years also brought about the demise of the forests. Virtually all the virgin red and white pines, some said to be over 200 feet tall, were felled. Logging and fires have drastically altered the North Shore's appearance. Today, there are no stands of virgin pines remaining.

MINING:

At the same time the lumber industry was flourishing, rich iron ore deposits were discovered inland near Lake Vermillion in 1865. Speculators came to Minnesota from the East and West Coasts. Jay Cooke, Carnegie, J.P. Morgan, and the Merritt Brothers raced to pocket the wealth. A total of 400 mines on Minnesota's three iron ranges (Vermillion, Mesabi, and Cuyana) produced the ore that helped meet most of growing America's demand for steel.

Iron ore was sent by railway car to the ports of Duluth and Two Harbors and loaded onto freighters that traveled down the Great Lakes to the steel mills in Cleveland, Pittsburgh, and Buffalo. This valuable resource was not limitless, however, and by the 1950s, all the high-grade iron ore had been mined. The mining industry declined briefly until new plants were built that could process the low-grade taconite ore.

FISHING:

The first permanent residents of the North Shore were Norwegian fishermen, who settled in the late 1800s near the mouths of rivers. By 1900, there were hundreds of fishermen making a living from the North Shore fishery, catching lake trout, whitefish, and siscowet trout. When the trout and whitefish declined, North Shore fishermen pulled more than five million pounds of herring from the lake each year. Today, there are only a few licensed commercial fishermen left in this area.

TOURISM:

Upon completion of U.S. Highway 61 in 1925, the isolated North Shore communities were opened to the rest of the nation. Many of the old commercial fishing camps became rustic summer resorts for tourists. The scenic beauty of the North Shore attracts increasing numbers of visitors.

There are four kinds of trout in Lake Superior and its tributaries. Which one is this?

LAKE TROUT. Look at the pictures of other kinds of trout. Can you tell the difference? The following descriptions will help you.

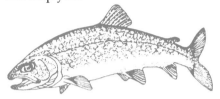

Lake Trout

Salvelinus namaycush

Length: 24-40 inches

Weight: 4-22 pounds

Coloring: light spots on darker background; light underside

Common names: Great Lakes trout, laker, namaycush, togue, grey trout, mountain trout

These swift, torpedo-shaped predators are native to most cold regions of the North American continent, but life in the Great Lakes has not been easy for the lake trout.

Around the upper lakes, sawmill wastes and other forms of pollution long ago drove the lake trout from their spawning streams. Like the lake whitefish, some adapted to this by spawning on offshore reefs and shoals.

In the early 1900s, lake trout became the most valuable commercial fish in the Great Lakes and remained so for almost 50 years. Then in the 1950s, the sea lamprey ruthlessly sought out these large, meaty fish as their prime victims.

Sea lamprey controls and vigorous stocking programs are now enabling lake trout to make a comeback. After planting, most lake trout stay within a 50-mile radius of the planting site, although some migrate up to 300 miles. Like salmon, lake trout have a strong homing instinct, returning to

spawn at planting sites or nearby streams. However, they have not had much success reproducing in Lake Superior.

Today, there are three distinctive kinds of lake trout in Lake Superior: the most typical, the salmon-like "lean" trout, found inshore; the 'fat' lake trout, which stays in deeper waters; and the 'jumper,' a deep-bodied, short-headed variety which hovers offshore near shoals and reefs.

Brown Trout

Salmo trutta

Length: 15-28 inches

Weight: 1-9 pounds

Coloring: light brown or tawny black, becoming silvery on the sides and belly

Common names: brownie, German brown trout, German trout, European brown trout, breac

Brown trout, a European relative of the Atlantic salmon, came to North America back in 1883. In that year, Michigan introduced them to her waters, and Wisconsin followed suit just four years later.

Although judged inferior by some to brook and rainbow trout, this resourceful immigrant eventually proved itself able to grow faster, live longer and adjust to degraded habitats not suitable to the other two trout.

Typically a stream fish, the brown trout also manages well in large lakes. Wild stocks are reproducing in Canadian and southwestern regions of Lake Superior. Brown trout in Lake Superior live around five or six years and spawning first occurs in late autumn of the third year of life.

This usually takes place at the gravelly headwaters of a stream and sometimes on rocky reefs along shore.

Fishermen can be considered the chief predators of the adult brown trout, although they are among the wariest of fish, feeding usually at dusk or at night. In 1971 a record brown trout–near 30 pounds– was taken from the lake. In many localities surf casting for brown trout is rapidly gaining popularity.

Brook Trout

Salvelinus fontinalis

Length: 11-15 inches

Weight: 12-24 pounds

Coloring: olive-green to dark brown on back; lighter sides; silvery white underside

Common names: Eastern brook trout, speckled trout, coaster, aurora trout, square-tall, sea trout

The brook trout is the only stream-dwelling trout native to the Great Lakes region. In search of clear, cool and well-oxygenated water, brook trout often move out of the streams and into the more desirable estuaries and bays of the Great Lakes. In these areas, they are called "coasters."

These tasty trout grow quickly on a smorgasboard of living organisms-everything from mayflies to salamanders. At an optimum temperature of 55°F, coasters have been found to consume 50 percent of their own weight in minnows weekly.

On average, coasters weigh two to three pounds and are usually heavier than the stream-dwelling brook trout. The largest brook trout on record was caught in Ontario province's Nipigon River and weighed 14.5 pounds, a record that has stood since 1915.

Although natural populations of brook trout reside in Lake Superior, Minnesota and Wisconsin are also stocking several thousand each year to help maintain the "coaster" variety as well as the stream-dwelling native. This benefits such predators as kingfishers and mergansers, not to mention the appreciative sports fishermen.

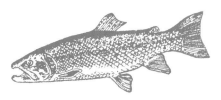

Rainbow Trout

Salmo gairdneri

Length: 15-28 inches

Weight: 1-9 pounds

Coloring: steel-blue, blue-green, yellow-green to almost brown on back; silvery sides; silvery white below

Common names: steelhead trout, coast rainbow trout, silver trout

This attractive game fish, leaping valiantly to dislodge the hook, is the sports fisherman's joy.

The first rainbow trout, planted in the Great Lakes in 1895, were probably of the Pacific "steelhead" variety. This strain migrates to the ocean before returning to spawn in their home streams. After the young fry emerge from the gravel spawning beds, they remain in the home stream at least 14 months and then migrate to open water as smolts. Biologists believe this life cycle enables the steelhead to adapt to the Great Lakes, moving in and out of the inland seas much as they would the ocean.

Rainbow trout can be easily located in the lake as they swim along the coast seldom deeper than 35 feet. In their wanderlust they range widely. Tagging has revealed that some trout, planted in Lakes Michigan and Huron, migrate as far north as the

Canadian shores of Lake Superior. Conversely, rainbow trout planted in the Brule and other western tributaries of Lake Superior have been recovered in Lakes Michigan and Huron.

Unlike Pacific salmon, which die after spawning, rainbow trout survive to spawn two or more times. As a result, the future of this popular fish in the Great Lakes is bright, particularly in Lake Superior, which has many fine spawning streams for trout.

Why are caribou no longer found in Minnesota?

A combination of factors caused caribou to disappear from Minnesota: overhunting, logging, and the appearance of the white-tailed deer. Woodland caribou are migratory animals that once roamed throughout Canada, the Northern Rockies, Upper Great Lakes, and New England. These deer prefer mature pine forests. As the southern parts of their range were altered by logging, the caribou migrated northward to more forested areas.

Once the virgin timber was removed, young trees appeared, providing an ideal habitat for the white-tailed deer. In Minnesota, the white-tailed deer began to flourish at the turn of the century. White-tailed deer are carriers of a parasitic roundworm, which resides in the deers' brain. Although harmless to its white-tailed host, the parasite is deadly to caribou and moose.

Another factor was overhunting. Caribou were once a major source of meat and hides for the Indians and early European settlers.

No caribou were seen in Minnesota after 1935 until a few were sighted north of Grand Marais in 1981. These caribou apparently strayed down from Canada. Wildlife experts don't know if caribou will be able to re-establish themselves in Minnesota.

Why are the waters of some North Shore streams the color of root beer?

Most of the streams emptying into Lake Superior have their origins no more than twenty miles inland. These streams start flowing from wetlands that support a wide variety of plant life, including cattails, marsh grasses, sphagnum moss, and tamarack trees. These plants release tannin, which colors the water.

How are the potholes formed in the lava rock near waterfalls?

Potholes in the lava rock near waterfalls are "tooled" out of the rock by loose pebbles and boulders that are swirled by the force of the water.

Why do deer congregate along the shore in winter?

Because of its size, the lake influences the local weather, acting as an air conditioner in the summer and a radiator of warmth (especially when it is not frozen) in the winter.

Milder temperatures and less snow along the shore attract deer. They congregate in three-mile-wide "deer yards" along the shore. The deer can frequently be seen along the highway.

Today, the fish population of Lake Superior is only a fraction of what it once was. Why?

Three major factors have contributed to the decline of Lake Superior's fish population: pollution, overfishing, and the introduction of exotic fish species.

Pollution:

Pollution has not had as great an impact in Lake Superior as it has on the lower Great Lakes. But pollution, especially from the pulp and paper industries, probably ruined prime spawning habitat for some fish species in industrial areas. Fish have also been contaminated with such toxic organic chemicals as DDT, PCB, and toxaphene. Recently, it has been found that most of these toxic chemicals come from the atmosphere.

Overfishing:

Overfishing has affected many of the more commercially valuable fish in Lake Superior. Improvements in fishing gear, boats, and techniques place increased stress on fish populations. Commercial fishing has now been limited by many regulations that set commercial fishing harvest below levels that will harm fish populations.

Exotic Species:

Introduction of exotic fish species (together with fishing pressure and pollution of spawning grounds) has had the greatest impact on Lake Superior fish populations. Perhaps the most serious change occurred when the sea lamprey worked its way from the Atlantic Ocean into all of the Great Lakes. This primitive, jawless fish attaches to the side of other fish with its suction-type mouth, rasps a hole, and feeds on the victim's blood and body fluids. Lamprey decimated stocks of lake trout and whitefish in the 1950s. A chemical control program has since reduced lamprey numbers.

Another addition to Lake Superior is smelt, also an ocean fish. When smelt became abundant in Lake Superior, herring, which was the most abundant species, became scarce.

Ruffe

Improvements in shipping have meant an increase in invading species from Europe. Zebra mussels, ruffe, and spiny water flea have all reached Lake Superior in the ballast water of ocean-going ships. Scientists continue to study the effect these new species will have on Lake Superior's fragile ecosystem.

Zebra Mussel

Why, in Summer, do rivers in the southern part of the North Shore, such as the Gooseberry and Baptism Rivers, run more slowly then those in the northern part?

The headwaters of the southern rivers are not as large as those of the northern rivers. During the summer, the source waters of these southern rivers almost dry up, leaving a small stream where a large river once was. The source waters of the northern rivers are located in the water-rich Boundary Waters Canoe Area.

Who were the voyageurs?

The voyageurs, mostly Frenchmen from Northern Canada and the Montreal area, were a stocky, adventuresome, and proud group that often paddled their canoes 15 hours a day on their journeys. Each May, groups of Voyageurs known as porkeaters (salted pork was a staple in their diet) would leave Montreal in flotillas of canoes that were filled with pots, pans, knives, guns, etc., to be used in barter. At the same time, another group of Voyageurs, known as northmen, would leave wilderness trading posts in canoes filled with 90 pound packs of furs that had been trapped by the Indians the preceding winter and spring. Both groups would meet, or rendezvous, at Grand Portage in August to exchange their goods and to celebrate.

CREDITS

This book was written in 1986 by Eugene D. Gennaro and Nancy Hereid with research assistance from Allen D. Glenn and Steven Rakow. Contributors included: Gerald C. Backlund, Bruce H. Munson, and Mary Jo Olson.

It was updated and revised by Sea Grant staff in 1993.

Alice Tibbetts and Ellen Shriner, editors

Linda Larson, designer

Third printing, 1993.

Published by Minnesota Sea Grant
NA90AA-D-SG149

 Sea Grant is a statewide program that supports research, education, and extension programs related to Lake Superior and Minnesota's water resources. It is part of the National Sea Grant College Program, which supports programs in 29 coastal and Great Lakes states.

Sea Grant is funded by the National Oceanic and Atmospheric Administration, the state legislature, and the University of Minnesota.

The University of Minnesota is an equal opportunity employer and educator.

PHOTO CREDITS:

Department of Natural Resources: 6, 9, 10, 17, 19

Michael Douglas: 2, 36

Duluth News Tribune: 4, 15

Linda Larson: 1, 14, 16, 26, 45

Rob Levine: 13, 31, 33, 41

Ryck Lydecker: 35

Minnesota Department of Tourism: cover, 25, 45

Minnesota Historical Society: 7, 8, 9, 11, 20, 22, 23, 24, 43

Minnesota Sea Grant: 12, 16

Sher Stonemann: 14, 21, 35, 39, 40

Caroline Tibbetts: 33

University of St. Thomas: 44

TEXT CREDITS:

University of Wisconsin Sea Grant, Fish of Lake Superior, pages 50-52.

RESOURCE LIST

For more information on Lake Superior, request these items from Sea Grant.

____**The Seiche Newsletter.** Covers the research, extension, and educational activities of Minnesota Sea Grant plus issues related to Lake Superior and the environment. Published four times a year. Free. SEN

____**Recreation and Weather Guide to the Minnesota Shore of Lake Superior.** Facts and figures about temperature and weather conditions on Lake Superior and on Minnesota's North Shore. 32 pp. Free. T1

____**The Edge of the Arrowhead.** Thumbnail sketches tell the history of Minnesota's North Shore. 60 pp. $2.00/$1.50 bulk. T2

____**Weather Wisdom of the North Shore.** How to use North Shore conditions to forecast the weather. Free. T4

____**The Fisheries of the Great Lakes.** Explains the reasons for dramatic changes in the lakes' fisheries from a natural fishery to one maintained by stocking. Outlines the reasons for the decline of the lake trout and exploding populations of alewives and smelt. $2.00. F1

____**Fish of Lake Superior.** Descriptions and illustrations of the fish found in the lake. Free. F2

____**Fish Contaminants.** Bibliography of materials for the general public and researchers on fish contaminants in the Great Lakes. Includes materials from six Great Lakes Sea Grant programs. Free. F6

____**The Sea Lamprey:** Invader of the Great Lakes. The lamprey's life history, its effect on the lakes' fisheries, and control efforts. Free. X6

____**A Field Guide to Aquatic Exotic Plants and Animals.** Features photos, drawings, and descriptions of ruffe, zebra mussels, spiny water flea, Eurasian watermilfoil, purple loosestrife, plus brief descriptions of carp, lamprey, rusty crayfish, white perch, flowering rush, and curly-leaf pondweed. Ten pages, four-fold. Free. X9

____**Hypothermia: The Cold Facts.** A half-hour broadcast-quality videotape that explains how to prevent hypothermia and increase your chances of surviving a fall into cold water. This award-winning program explains why some people tolerate the cold longer than others, how your attitude affects your ability to survive, and how your body protects you from the cold. Available in VHS or Beta. $20.00. B1

____**Survival in Cold Water: Hypothermia Prevention.** Fact sheet describes symptoms of hypothermia, survival at various water temperatures, and how to increase survival time. Free. B2

____**Scuba Diving the Minnesota Shore of Lake Superior.** Diving attractions along the lake. What divers can see at each site. Free. B4

____**Fixin Fish: A Guide to Handling, Buying, Preserving, and Preparing Fish.** Shows you how to get the best from your catch by handling it properly to keep it fresh and preparing it well. Recipes and ideas for cooking, pickling, and smoking all kinds of fish. Explanations of fish parasites and how to remove them are included. $6.95. C1

____**Kitchi Gami Cookery: A Primer on Lake Superior Fish.** 30 recipes. $2.00 retail/$1.50 bulk. C2

____Smelt-Dip Net to Dish. How to handle, clean, store and prepare smelt; 11 recipes. Free. C6

____Fish Oil and Your Health. Fish is low in fat and cholesterol and high in protein. This fact sheet explains why fish oil helps prevent heart attacks by reducing blood clotting. Free. C8

Check the publications you want and return form. Orders must be prepaid.

Make checks payable to University of Minnesota.

Minnesota Sea Grant Publications
University of Minnesota
1518 Cleveland Ave N #302
St. Paul, MN 55108
(612) 625-9288
Fax: (612) 625-1253

- -

ORDER FORM:

I got this Family Guide from:

__ The Seiche   __ Resort
__ Publication list   __ Magazine (please list)
__ Bookstore   __ Other
__ Park

NAME: _____

ADDRESS _____

CITY _____ STATE _____ ZIP _____

TOTAL COST $ _____

Make checks payable to: University of Minnesota